HOUSES OF GOLD

JOHN CARDEN CAMPBELL

HOUSES OF GOLD

PHOTOGRAPHS: **CRAIG BUCHANAN**

SPECIAL PHOTO SECTION: MORLEY BAER

FOREWORD: DONALD BIGGS

MAPS: DAVID RICHARDSON

SAN DIEGO   Howell -North Books   CALIFORNIA

First Edition
Manufactured in the United States of
America

For information write to:

Howell North Publishers, Inc.
11175 Flintkote Avenue,
San Diego, CA 92121

Library of Congress Cataloging in Publication Data

Campbell, John Carden.
  Houses of gold.

  1. Architecture, Domestic—California.
2. Architecture, Modern—19th
century—California. 3. Dwellings—
California. I. Title.

NA7235.C2C35   728.3′7′09794   80-21299
ISBN 0-8310-7121-4

1 2 3 4 5 6 7 8 9 84 83 82 81 80

Contents

Acknowledgments

Few of us work alone—so we enlist the help of interested persons, in varying degrees—I thus wish to express my fullest appreciation to all those listed below and some who helped anonymously.

However, special credits and thanks must be extended to three women whose tireless efforts helped make this book possible: Marie Louise Hughes, Margaret Hart, and Betty Gardiner

Others are listed by individual names, not organizations, and for the area in which they were helpful: Robert and Marilyn Judd, Sonora; Rodney and Bonnie Brooks, Sonora; Sharon Marovich, Sonora; Judith Cunningham, San Andreas; Harold Kauffman, San Andreas; Jason McCord, San Andreas; Irma Schrag, Mokelumne Hill; Marge Pease, Jackson; Marian Watry, Placerville; Kathleen Todd, Placerville; Marjorie and Fritz Blodgett, Auburn; Lardner-Lardner Arch., AIA, Auburn; Carol and David Fluke, Nevada City; David Osborn, Nevada City; Charles Woods, Nevada City; Robert Wyckoff, Nevada City; John Seaver, all areas; Hugh Mayrand, all areas.

Foreword

If the houses of gold in John Carden Campbell's title were not precisely *of* gold, they are all situated along California State Highway 49 in that area known as California's Gold Country. Part of that area, from Sonora northward to Auburn, is on California's geographical Mother Lode—the mineral-rich Mother Lode of Gold.

California and gold are virtually synonymous. The origin of its name? From medieval Spanish legend for an island of gold, but more of that later. As New York is the Empire and Texas the Lone Star, California is The Golden State. California's state flower is the golden poppy. California's official state fish? Yes, state fish—the Golden Trout. On the Great Seal of the State of California adopted in 1849, a miner works with pick and shovel against the backdrop of the gold country, under the single-word California State Motto—"Eureka" —from the Greek *heurēka,* an interjection expressing triumph at finding or discovering something desirable. Gold, of course. These things matter.

If Campbell's carefully selected houses are not really of gold, neither did the stream beds of the Sierra Nevada run with gold "to the thickness of a man's hand," as reported by effusive writers in New York newspapers in late 1848. With greater authority and glittering evidence to boot, President James K. Polk in his December 1848 farewell message was informing Congress that in California "the accounts of the abundance of gold are of such an extraordinary character as would scarcely command belief were they not corroborated." (Right then 230 ounces of California gold on display at the War Department were drawing excited crowds. Samples, according to the Philadelphia Mint, had a degree of fineness equal to the standard of United States gold coins.)

Polk had determinedly acquired California, promising to take it by force if necessary as he campaigned for election in 1844; in 1846 he did so. It was appropriate then that he should be the American President to announce discovery of golden treasure in a California newly in the possession of the United States. For three centuries California had been Spanish territory, for a quarter of a century Mexican. In February 1848, the American-occupied territory of California was formally acquired by treaty from Mexico at the end of an almost effortless war. This occurred nine days after the discovery of gold—both related and curiously unrelated events. The terrible and noteworthy irony is that the Spaniards had discovered the treasures of Mexico and Peru, but had entirely failed to find gold in California. California's very name had originated in a popular fifteenth century chivalric romance published in Seville. In it was written: "there is an island named California, very close to that part of the Terrestrial Paradise, which is inhabited by black women. . . . Their weapons were all made of gold. The island everywhere abounds with gold and precious stones, and upon it no other metal was found." Cortés carried this book, among others, into Mexico in the 1519–1521 conquest. Cortés himself wrote the Spanish King about the rumored island abounding in gold. (Spanish explorers still believed the long peninsula we know as Lower California to be an island.) No one knows who first named the province California, but the riches and especially the gold of the fabled island were anticipated.

Spanish exploration of California was superficial. Centuries after the beginning of Spanish settlement, dating from about 1770, the mission, presidio and pueblo system was confined almost entirely to the coast. Notice that of the twenty-one missions, none is very far inland. As the eighteenth century drew to an end, the sparse population of Spaniards and their Mexican successors were interested almost exclusively in grazing land. The Sierra and its foothills, with their golden secrets, were of little interest; they were distant and rather forbidding and above all unnecessary.

Americans had an appetite for land, a "boa-constrictor appetite" as one congressman graphically described it in 1846. Throughout the nineteenth century the American flag had followed the American people westward. In the 1840s the American people were settling in Oregon and California, the continent's end, and axiomatically the American flag and the American military followed. Then came the two portentous events of 1848, the gold discovery on January 24 and the cession of California to the United States on February 2. In the next five years, life in California underwent a more profound transformation than at any other time in the state's history.

Changes were radical. One reliable historian fairly estimates the total population of California in 1848 (excluding Indians) at a maximum of 15,000, many of whom had already been lured from Mexico and the Pacific Basin to work in the gold fields. The Seventh Federal Census in 1850 showed California as having grown to 93,000, a figure everyone agreed was ridiculously low—so low that a state census was authorized in 1852. If simple numbers do not lie, California in 1852 had a population of 260,000. San Francisco's population grew from approximately 700 in mid-1848 to a city of 40,000 in mid-1850. The boom was on; the Gold Rush had happened.

Another fine California historian, using an appropriate figure from architecture, has called gold "the cornerstone" of the state. Records of gold production in 1848 were not kept with any accuracy, but gold production in 1849 approximated $10,000,000; in 1850, $41,000,000; in 1851, $76,000,000; and in 1852, $81,000,000. A substantial cornerstone. In the century after the discovery, California's output of gold totaled about two billion dollars. Gold influenced California's history more than any other single factor.

There in the western foothills of the Sierra Nevada was one of the richest, most accessible gold regions in the world and gold gathering was rather easy for the first few years. This was fortunate for the early

Argonauts, as they quickly came to be called (likened to the followers of Jason in his quest for the Golden Fleece), because they were woefully untrained and ill equipped for "mining." They were a cosmopolitan bunch and if they had come to exploit, get rich quick and return home—the East, the South or Europe—many changed their plans. Some could not afford to leave; others chose not to. The resultant society in California was fascinating—one of the more remarkable and one of the most democratic societies on earth.

Somewhere in his voluminous writings on California history, H. H. Bancroft calls the gold rush year of 1849 "an exclamation point in the history of civilization. . . . Not so much an episode as an era." There is something to what he says. Consider an obvious, but often overlooked, fact of the Gold Rush. The Argonauts came to California from somewhere where they had followed trades and professions. They brought these skills (and often their tools) with them to California. Well that they did, too, because only a fraction of them made the rich gold strikes they dreamed of, which is not to say that they did not prosper.

The point is most dramatically shown, by way of specific example, in the 800-plus men in Col. Jonathan D. Stevenson's volunteer New York regiment. President Polk sent the regiment of citizen-soldiers to conquer California in late 1846, assuming they would remain as the vanguard of American colonization. These men were on the spot in 1848 for the beginning of the epidemic "gold fever." Many of them were among the first in the "diggings." Just as few of them had been soldiers before enlistment in the regiment, none had been a miner.

A quick look at some of their civilian occupations before coming to California is illuminating and most relevant to John Campbell's discussion of Gold-Country houses. In one of the ten regimental companies there were: professional men (including a physician and a surgeon), metal tradesmen (including a tin roofer), white-collar workers, farmers, followers of many miscellaneous trades and services, and—note this—ten building tradesmen. The tradesmen included four carpenters, two cabinetmakers, one sash maker, two masons and one stone finisher. In another of the ten companies, in addition to blacksmiths, tinsmiths, surveyors and locksmiths, there were fourteen building tradesmen—three carpenters, two cabinetmakers, two moulders, two plasterers, one varnisher, two masons and two painters. The building trades were at least as well represented in the other eight companies.

Many of these men spent years in the Gold Country, and no fewer than ten percent spent the rest of their lives there. Add to these craftsmen from Stevenson's Regiment the building tradesmen from the tens of thousands of other men who swarmed into the gold country and it is no real wonder that surviving Gold-Country buildings are far from primitive. Depending on the area, there was good stone to quarry, good clay for bricks, abundant timber almost everywhere and lots of rivers and streams to provide ample water for sawmills. (James Marshall's 1848 gold discovery had been made as he was supervising construction of a sawmill on the American River at present-day Coloma.)

The houses pictured here were not the first dwellings in any of these communities; they were not simply shelters. Many of them built in the 1850s were clearly built for permanence. Designed with taste and style (often several styles combined), they were not solely utilitarian. The ideal of what a house should look like was one of many factors that determined their shapes.

Some of the architectural and structural ideas were in the builders' heads. Some new Californians wanted to re-create their childhood or early adulthood homes in the East. (Some few actually imported prefabricated structures, although fewer Gold-Country houses came overland or "'round the Horn" than is rumored.) Most of the architectural ideas represented in these houses came from books. The Gold Rush brought a flourishing book trade to California in 1849, most certainly including illustrated architecture books and carpenters' manuals. Just as these books had carried structural ideas and forms from the Eastern seaboard into the back country, now they carried mid-nineteenth century building and decorating concepts directly to California, skipping the slow process of evolution. A perfect example is one of John Campbell's favorite houses of his youth and of his maturity, the Doric-columned house in Mokelumne Hill. Where nothing had stood in 1850 (or at best a tent, shack or lean-to), in 1853 rose a geometrical, symmetrical gem of a house, its design informed by an intellectual concept of neoclassicism. It is as practical and perfect for the altitude and climate as its rational geometry is touched by grace.

Its source? One or another or several books in which carpenters could find details of structure and ornament. These books came in personal libraries, with carpenters, with booksellers. They carried such titles as: *Rudiments of Architecture, The Practical House Carpenter, Elements of Architecture, The Builder's Guide, Cottage Residences, The Architecture of Country Houses.* From them, builders could copy or adapt to serve the owners' wishes and budgets. Some great houses were produced and some remain, but most were not baronial. They were, rather, practical and at the same time refined dwellings for ordinary people. Notice that in general those that survived longest sat furthest from "downtown." Then imagine what these gold-country towns looked like in their heyday. They looked fine indeed.

The subject of buildings and of houses in the Gold Country is hardly untouched, but the treatment of these selected houses by designer-author John Carden Campbell enlightens us with his informed and personal point of view. If the carpenters' manuals referred to above were "how-to" books, and they were, this eye-opening volume is just what the author calls it—a "look book." Recipient of dozens of awards from federal and state agencies, professional societies, historical and preservation groups, John Carden Campbell is known internationally for his building design and for his efforts in historical preservation.

This foreword has alluded to the powerful and persuasive nature of books, from the fanciful Spanish yarn that gave California its name to the practical builders' guides that gave California's Gold-Country houses their look. In the present book we welcome the critical and appreciative eye of John Carden Campbell focused on his choice *Houses of Gold*.

Donald C. Biggs
San Francisco
March 28, 1980

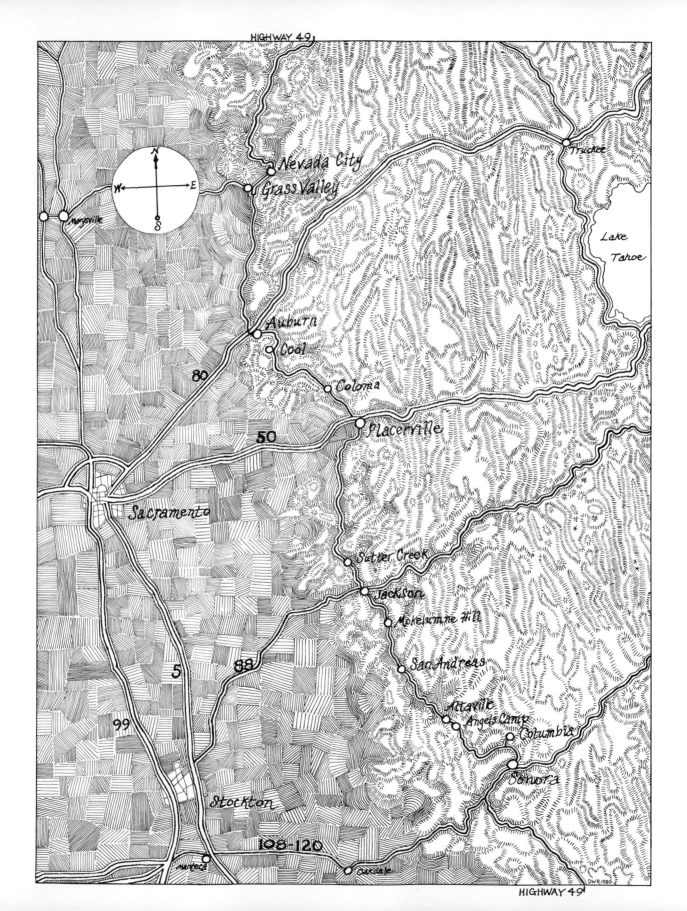

HIGHWAY 49,

Houses of Gold

HOUSES OF GOLD were not made of gold, but they were surely a direct product of the affluence created by that precious yellow metal that was mined first in ditches and holes in the ground's surface and later by machinery and mine shafts going deep into the earth. No matter how it was wrung out of the land, gold flowed for years, and because of it, stable communities of homes and businesses grew up. Today, we can still see and enjoy the HOUSES OF GOLD built in California during those first fifty years of gold mining.

HOUSES OF GOLD is primarly a "LOOK BOOK"—a look at history for the pleasure of seeing how our forebears lived and what they built. We will not look at what the world would call "great architecture" but rather at buildings with a simple handsomeness that we can now cherish. They are a gift to us from the 19th century and remain a remarkable record of that time; in their survival, that era did not stop after the gold ran out, but has become a continuing part of the 20th century.

This look at California history covers roughly the years from 1850 to 1900, from the earliest houses built in the Gold Country to the end of the Victorian period. From the 1920s on, too little of architectural interest was produced to continue to record it. The primary interest of this book is to select houses in the Gold Country that were built after the mad stampede for gold in the late 1840s and that illustrate the variety, richness, dignity—and often elegance—of home building in those years.

This tour through the Gold Country concentrates only on houses and makes no attempt to comment on other building types—stores, firehouses, hotels, churches. Houses are built to become homes; they are just buildings until they provide shelter and privacy for a family, encouraging the most intimate and rewarding of human relationships. The privacy of a house makes it a refuge, a sanctuary, a center for our most personal expressions. Without this privacy, we doubtless would all be at loose ends, wanderers—(as were most of the early miners). So, we have focused on houses because they symbolize the settling and stabilizing of an area through a love expressed in building homes for families.

No attempt has been made to date every house shown. We are more interested in your seeing these houses of the Gold Country as a new, special expression of architecture between 1850 and 1900: part New England, part Italian, part Spanish, but all adapted to the California climate in the Sierra foothills and to the way of life in the latter-19th century.

We will stay in areas that are on Route 49 and its immediate surroundings, from Sonora in the south to Nevada City in the north. Houses of interest are to be seen north and south of these two points, but the richest viewing is between Sonora and Nevada City. Thus, you can see most of the best houses on a simple route, and you do not have to go off uncharted byways to find them. Several maps are included to guide you into particular areas. When you get an overall sense of one locality, you can see individual houses as they relate to others built at different times.

Sonora, Jackson, Placerville, Auburn, Grass Valley and Nevada City, incidentally, never became "ghost towns," but have remained active, growing communities. A look at their development through the years, in contrast to other communities, prompts us to examine concepts of "growth" and "change," especially as they relate to preservation of our historic buildings. Obviously, growth and change are basic to man's development and affect us all. Some embrace change with wild enthusiasm; others resist it with a passion, but change we do. If we accept change as natural to human beings, we can have a fuller appreciation of the houses and towns we see along Route 49. Some went all out to keep up and be "modern." Some went into decay and disappeared. Others, like Sonora and Nevada City, struggled with the problems of growing and at the same time retained some basic values that were important in their past.

Nevada City is one of the best examples of a community that managed to relate the new with the old while the town grew and times changed. In the changes from the 1850s on, a continuous process of adaptation, representing a whole range of styles and building types, is evident. Individual houses and buildings of all kinds date from 1850 to 1970: the simple, elegant Freeman-Marling House on Nevada Street; Victorian houses; 1920s houses; even two classic examples of "1930 modern"—city Hall on Broad Street and the tall "Radio City Modern" 1930s County Courthouse, with its very contemporary glass-walled addition built in the 1960s.

A recent expression of relating new and old in Nevada City is the Bank of America, an excellent example of building "new" while not copying the "old"; it is brick, with small windows, and has a strong massive feeling that is very sympathetic to the existing buildings but is not a slavish, bad copy. (In contrast, the architect of the Wells Fargo Bank in Grass Valley tried to copy the "old"; this bank is full of false windows and does not give a true feeling of the Gold Country building style.) And of course, Nevada City today has a car wash, gas station and antique shops—building types that didn't exist during the Gold Rush (when no one even imagined having a car or thought of selling off old furniture and possessions as precious objects to use and treasure).

HOUSES OF GOLD, then, can lead you to new discoveries. Follow the maps. In exploring California's recent past, you should find unexpected rewards.

SONORA

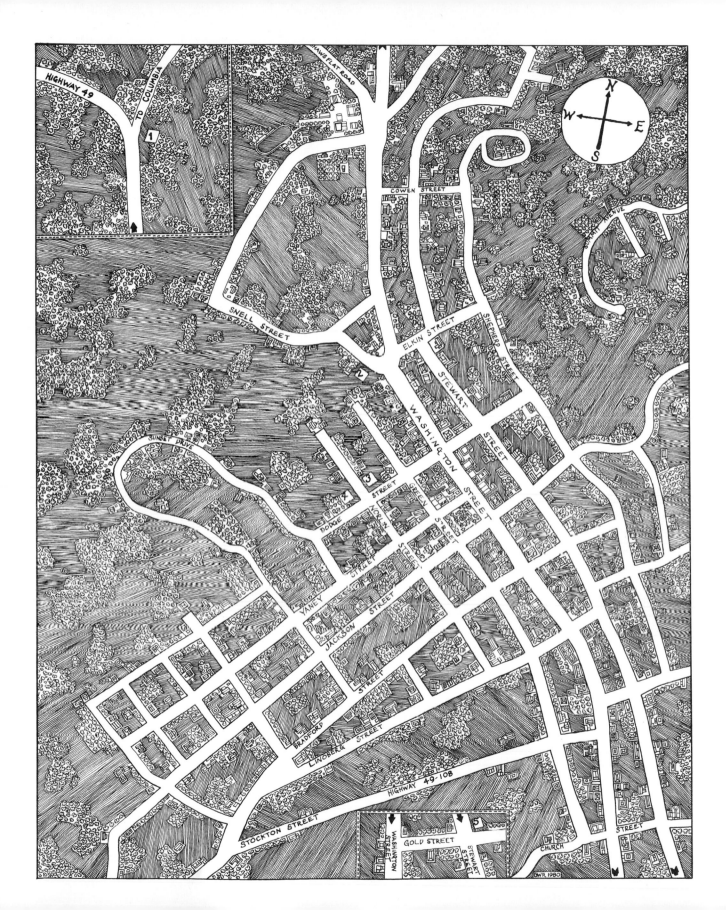

The Cady House

This charming, small (about 1,670 sq. ft.) house crowns a hill above the town of Sonora. It was prefabricated in Virginia and shipped around the Horn. Built in 1856 by John S. Cady, a hardware merchant who came to California in 1852, it has been in the family since and is still owned by his descendants.

I find this one of the classics of its period. The plan will show you how the house was organized around the side porch, now shaded by the huge old oak and doubtless this was where outdoor living happened. Note the huge 12 x 20 ft. kitchen and the equally large dining room, contrasted to the small parlor and sitting room. It is interesting to see on the plan that only one area was designated as a bedroom. Even today one bedroom in a 1,700 sq. ft. house is unusual. The pantry is a room that is no longer included in plans. The only bath, which was probably added later, is clear through the house and out off the back porch.

The house is fascinatingly different from today's thinking. We do not have pantries, very often not even a dining room, or a family room. Today the rear sitting room would probably be a second or third bedroom, and now we still do cross one room to get to another. The whole planning concept was different. Here, in order to get to the kitchen from the front door, you go through four other rooms, or outside on the porch. Also note the lack of closets. For all that presumed inconvenience, the house is one of the most charming in the Gold Country.

It is very easy to imagine spending a cool evening on that side porch, overlooking the nearby ravine. The detail around the doors and windows is similar to that of the Woods House of Mokelumne Hill, and the overall proportion of doors, posts and railings combine to make a most appealing house. One frequently recurring story about most houses of this vintage is that the parts (millwork) were brought "around the Horn." Mills producing fine woodwork were a later development. By the time we get to the 1880s and 1890s, woodworking mills were available everywhere. On the detail sheet, study the way in which the wood was milled to create very refined interiors—a far cry from the shacks that miners lived in five or six years before.

The Cady House, Sonora. The first house in this book is the Cady House, one of the most interesting in the Gold Country in terms of age, history and especially architecture. It is a simple Greek Revival structure very popular in the 1850s and 1860s. Many of the area's buildings were simple rectangles with some good detailing that made them Greek Revival, but inside they followed a more florid design idea with more elaboration and decoration in the Victorian style.

Greek Revival (sometimes called Classic Revival) in the gable ends and the pediment at the porch over the front door. Note, however, the capital on the columns are not Greek, but more of a simple carpentry solution.

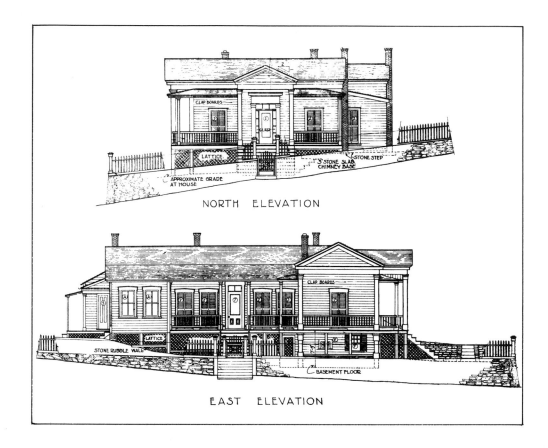

NORTH ELEVATION

EAST ELEVATION

When you look at these photos, relate them to the drawing done in the 1930s as a survey of historic buildings. It is interesting to see drawings come to life as real doors, windows, and walls.

A look across the front porch showing simple detail and variations in porch width. It would be hard to guess why the porch is narrower on one side than the other. Also note the scale of the siding—these narrow boards are a mark of that building period wherever you see it.

The front door (probably seldom used, since the side entrance is easier and more inviting) is formal and has pleasing proportions. The glass door shown in the 1930s drawing may be original, but it would seem more appropriate to have a multipaneled door, painted white or dark green.

A close look at the side porch shows a curved railing; it also shows an interesting variation on openings. There are three heights here, shown also on the drawing. Each indicates a different use of the interior space.

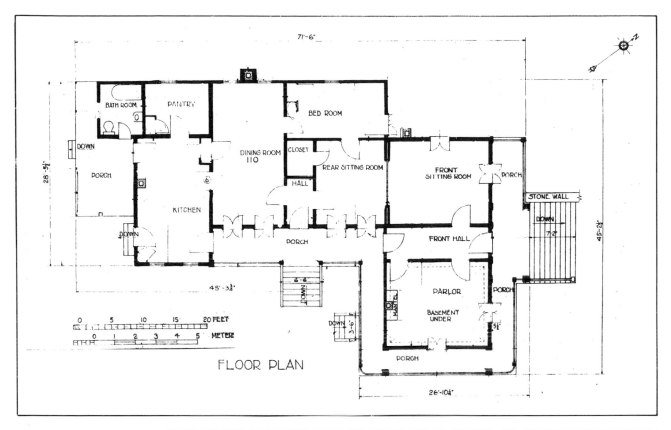

FLOOR PLAN

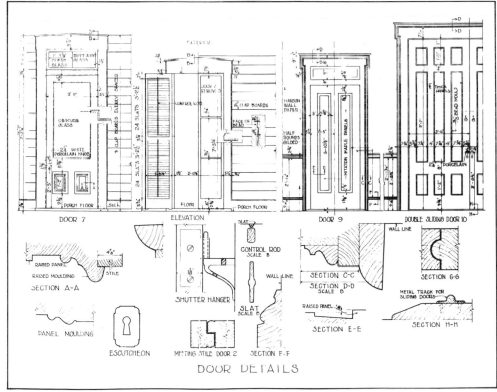

DOOR DETAILS

A close look at the porch. Here we can best see the tall elegantly
proportioned French doors surrounded by the classic trim
molding. Also note the door to the front hall is now closed up
and is a window.

This side entry is one of the most charming, attractive entries in the book, with the stone wall, the wide stair, the lattice, the oak tree with its lamp and then the wide porch.

An interior view showing the fine detail around windows and doors. This molding is very similar to the trim at the Mokelumne Hill House, but the wood is painted dark to imitate a finer grade. The wallpaper, in several patterns, is more sympathetic to Victorian ornateness.

A sawmill from around the late 1880s—a building of bold proportions related entirely to its use—looks like some contemporary houses of the 1980s.

A fragment of a house built in 1853—in Nevada City—may or may not be there still, but this photo shows a relation to a similar house in Sonora.

Some Thoughts on Preservation

While we are looking at these fine old houses, we must realize that part of their value is simply as living aspects of the past—actual three-dimensional structures, not merely two-dimensional illustrations in a book. The fact that they are here today to see and enjoy leads us to some thoughts on preservation.

Only a few short years ago the idea of preserving historic architecture either was not considered at all or was thought to be very low on the list of priorities for today's living. We have lost many a good house in favor of a parking lot, gas station or a motel. Ironically, many motels accommodate tourists who have come to see the very buildings that have been torn down to make room for more cars—a vicious cycle, to be sure.

Since we are newly, and often militantly, interested in saving our architectural heritage, some general ideas about preservation, restoration, reconstruction and even renewal need to be considered. First of all there are basically two approaches to preservation: (1) the museum approach, which is, of necessity, primarily educational and, (2) the commercial approach, which involves preserving an old building for new use—to live, eat, shop or work in.

Museum-quality preservation requires that authenticity be the most important consideration. The observer should be "told the truth" about what he sees and should get a true account of the life and times of the building. The Marsh-Christie House in Nevada City, preserved intact and furnished with much original furniture, is an example of such an approach. When you visit this house, you will be involved in a valid experience; you will share with its original owner a sense of the style, scale and sensitivity in design of the building.

On the other hand, the Classic Greek Revival home, the Woods House in Mokelumne Hill, was purchased by the author to be used for a weekend house. It was totally unfurnished and my friends and I, who came to enjoy it, surely did not want to use furniture thoroughly out of keeping with a newer lifestyle. Comfort and economy were more important than authenticity, so the furnishings selected were a mixture of old and new. Many aspects of the old house bring much pleasure in its new use: the covered porch, the elegant front doors, the high ceiling. But most important, in restoring it nothing was changed that would destroy the integrity of the original house. Walls and interior molding remain as they were. Even some of the old wallpaper was left in the hall, where it could be seen but not lived with; its drab color and ornate design made it unpleasant for use in a living area.

An appropriate remodeling was accomplished in the Bartlett House in Nevada City, a building very similar to the Marsh-Christie House (note the look-alike Belvederes). Here, the big porch apparently rotted off and was somehow removed. In the early 1970s, Mr. Bartlett remodeled a small porch roof, renewed the stairs, and generally made the porch relate better to the rest of the house. His renovations are not authentic in terms of the original structure, but they are in the spirit of the house and may be even more practical than the earlier large porch. In this case, use superseded authenticity and resulted in a respectable compromise between museum and commercial approaches. Discretion and taste are needed for renovating old buildings that have architectural merit and that are to be used for new purposes.

New buildings in an historic environment also should be given careful consideration in their design. They should not be slavish imitations or bad, impractical copies of the old, just to suggest historical authenticity. Few copies of old buildings are "authentic." The restoration of colonial Williamsburg, Virginia, is one of the very few examples of complete authenticity; buildings were restored or newly built from authentic old drawings, with exacting standards of perfection. Usually we don't have the money for that kind of "new" old building; moreover, today's use is probably quite different. The car wash in Nevada City, for example, is located in the historic zone, but certainly a car wash was not dreamed of in the 1850s or 1860s. This new building type, not a copy, was introduced into an historic area, yet it is not out of key with the rest of the buildings.

Use and re-use have many applications. An old store becomes a new restaurant; a foundry becomes a museum; a house becomes a store or an office; a factory becomes a shopping center; a post office becomes an arcade of shops, and so on. We can keep old buildings, with their aura of history, and still have usable buildings for new purposes.

We need not worship relics, but neither should we waste a valuable resource of buildings with a heritage. The restored "Old Town" in Sacramento (a good detour on your way to or from the Gold Country) is an excellent example of a pleasant place to shop or eat while thoroughly enjoying an historical area. Some changes have been made, but by and large the area is authentic. It could have been three times larger, but unfortunately, instead of routing a highway across the river through almost vacant land, highway officials sacrificed an historically rich part of the Sacramento area for freeway construction. Nevada City was similarly raped by the push for progress when a four-lane freeway, which could have stopped short of the city limits, was put through the center of town, cutting it in half. Most of Nevada City has thrived in spite of it—certainly not because of it.

**A street festival,
a festooned house, a
parade past the
Frank Street house.
The house was
light-colored then,
with dark trim,
and much decorated
for the occasion.
From the display of
flags, one might
assume it was the
Fourth of July 1900.**

Frank W. Street House, 19 West Snell Street, Sonora. Built in 1896. Designed by architect C. W. Ayers. A wonderfully complex sight and a wild variety of textures, railings, posts, porches, stained glass, varied forms. This house is probably the most ornate in the Gold Country. Its dark red color adds to the richness and reflects its period. If it were white, it would still be complex, but it wouldn't seem as Victorian. It is in full contrast to the simple (red) church across the street.

Double Bay: An interesting, but simple Victorian. The façade is symmetrical, instead of the more typical irregularity. The form is a simple box with two major bays and center porch, but the detail is all-Victorian—the turned posts, fancy pediment detail and turned railing—a handsome and dignified house.

Rosasco House, Sonora. Designed by architect C. W. Ayers. Again, Victorian, but white. The column caps are fanciful; the rail and other detail is as rich and varied as the period. The cupola with its different shingle patterns and iron rail at top add the usual asymmetrical touch. On this house, note the pediment on the porch— very much like one on the Cady house, but used in a totally different way.

One of the more restrained in Victorian style, a fanciful detail in the gable and roof form nicely graduated to the ground.

These ornate Victorian houses throughout the Gold Country reflect the change in time and style from earlier houses such as Cady House, O. T. Wood House and the Bernardi Building. The simpler ones were built in the 50s and 60s, the Victorians in the 80s and 90s, thus closing the century.

SONORA

The Nicol House. A massive, simple house, nicely detailed, pleasantly proportioned.

SONORA

A small house with lots of variety, as in the larger houses. There are nine different elements present, all wood, and repeated over the façade. The form is typically asymmetric.

❶

A house not distinguished for its detail, but a good example
of adapting house to climate. The three- to four-sided porches were
typical throughout the Gold Country. Here is a simple house
made more livable by the shade of the porches.

Here is a still simpler box. The detail is more Grecian
than Victorian, but the banding under the eaves takes it
into the Victorian.

ANGELS CAMP
ALTAVILLE
SAN ANDREAS
MOKELUMNE HILL
JACKSON
SUTTER CREEK

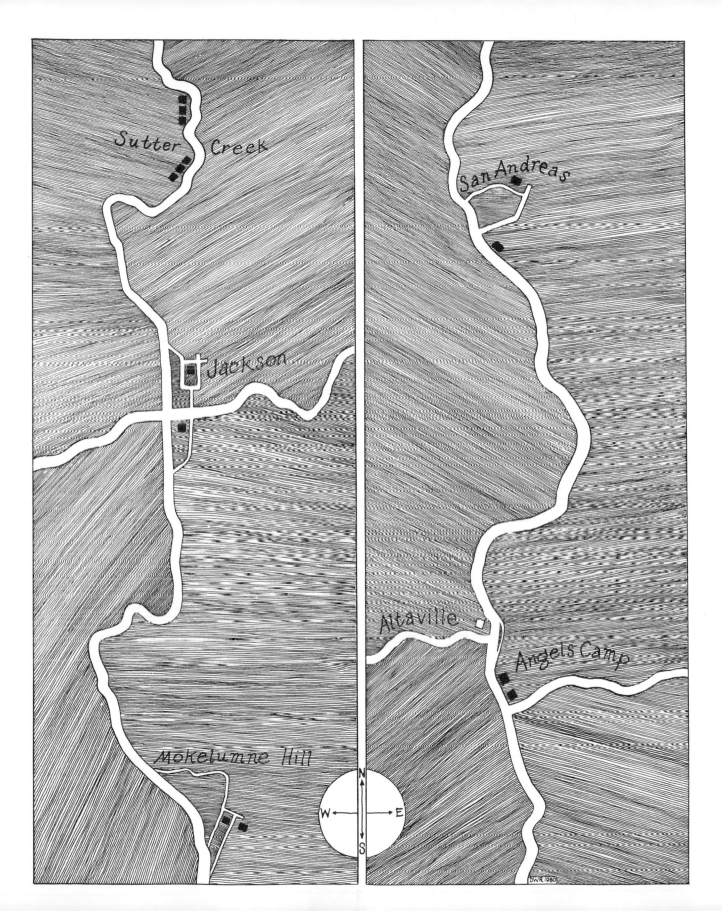

This Angels Camp house is one of the best on Highway 49.
Interesting in that it is built right on the street; one might
presume there was more space around it before the modern road
went through.

A small house that does not fit the pattern, yet is certainly
interesting. It is stone, covered in stucco, and it looks more like a
European farmhouse than post-Gold Rush houses.

Ben Thorne House, San Andreas. A house of bold brick
forms, with subordinate wooden details. A steep roof with icicles,
the porch, post and railing all enhance this basically simple
L-shaped house. Incidentally, this is one of the few brick houses
along Route 49; most of the rest are in wood.

Close-up of roof detail and the turned railing. Also note the cut-stone lintel over the window. The pattern is Greco-Roman as opposed to Gothic.

A beautiful curved stairway in the Victorian tradition. Many Victorian houses in San Francisco have this kind of stairway. Notice here that the stairway goes down as well as up—on the lower floor is the big, cool kitchen and dining combination. One side opens onto a garden and the opposite wall is dug into the ground and bricked.

The interior of the Ben Thorne house is nicely non-Victorian. If we are to use these fine old houses today, we need not feel obligated to live as the Victorians did. Here a mixture of Chinese screens, English antiques, Oriental rugs and other objects which simply suit the needs and desires of the present owners Harold Kaufmann and Jason McCord. It is appropriately tasteful and sympathetic to the old house, but does not attempt to be true to the period.

Yet another version of the asymmetrical Victorian in San Andreas,
but simpler in form than some of the others.

Modern History of One Old House

Throughout the Gold Country we can see many fine old houses, but several are outstanding and will be discussed in more detail:

Cady House—Sonora
Woods House—Mokelumne Hill
Tallon House—Jackson
Blair House—Placerville
Bernard House—Auburn
Coleman House—Grass Valley
Marling-Freeman House— Nevada City
Marsh-Christie House—Nevada City
Stewart House—Nevada City

The house built in 1853 by Dr. O. T. Woods is my particular favorite for various personal reasons. First, I once owned and restored it; but more than that, I feel it is a true classic. My personal connection with the house started in 1936. While on a sketching trip for college work in Sacramento, I discovered this gem of a small building (see sketch done from memory same year). Then, in 1939, I wanted to show some friends from Boston that we Westerners had some history too, so we journeyed to the Gold Country together. This time I photographed the house; these pictures (included for historical reasons and not for my photography) show the condition of the house at that time.

Nearly twenty years later, while on another tour through the Gold Country in 1958, I stopped in Mokelumne Hill and bought the old Odd Fellows Hall to use as a weekend place, only to discover that the Woods House was also for sale. The timing was fateful; I couldn't resist. So I bought it, too, and rented the Odd Fellows Hall for office space. (I also became involved in assembling a group to buy and re-store the old Leger Hotel—but that is another long story.)

The contours and elements of the Woods House are remarkably simple, corresponding to the three basic lines we all observe in design—the curve, the angle and the straight line; or the three basic forms—the pyramid, the cylinder and the cube.

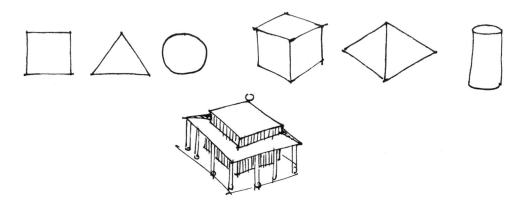

These three elements put together with skill and taste, plus some interesting detail, make what I regard as one of the most elegant small houses (five rooms) anywhere in the United States.

Why do I emphasize *small?* Because one rarely sees elegance or refinement in a small house, even today. The proportions are pleasing; the covered porch colonnade gives a handsome three-dimensional quality; and the details (ogee arches where the battens are brought together and the "icicle" wood detail under the eaves) seem just enough enrichment to add interest but not to overpower the basic forms—a restraint not achieved in later Victorian buildings.

Also of interest on the outside of the house are the basic unfinished porch floor and the lack of detail and finish by the stairs. This treatment seems somehow to be appropriately related to the real simplicity of the rest of the house. The underside of the roof on the porch is also unfinished, and this again adds to the charm of combining refined detail with unrefined finishing.

The finial is a modern touch—a gold-leafed sunburst. The house probably had a finial, but it was gone. We needed one to seal the point of the pyramid, so we ad-libbed and invented a new one (a gold sunburst, to express our pleasure in the old house, made of metal so it would not rot out). Note also in one picture how the roof pyramid seems to reflect the mountain peak in the distance.

Tall, stately French doors, rather than little holes punched in a box, add to the elegance of the house. Equally tall shutters repeat the proportion and are very functional, not just decorative. Incidentally, you may notice that the shutters by the front door do not seem big enough to close over the door; they are not, but they do function. They are built into the exterior wall, but glass windows behind them open, so that they act as ventilators for the hall—another example of the great sensitivity shown in the design of the whole house. The regular shutters close for privacy, light control and ventilation.

The structure itself sits on a foundation of piled-up rocks. Walls are two- by ten-inch planks laid vertically and joined with heavy battens. With two-inch thick walls, the interior is as described in historic accounts of early buildings: very rough, irregular slabs of wood of varying widths covered with heavy cloth gauze and then wallpapered. (The hall was not touched and still shows the original covering of the interior walls.)

The major rooms of the house are nicely proportioned. When I bought it the interior was fairly intact, except in the rear, where the kitchen and the bath were added (see plan). Inside features are the handsome door and the corridor trim in Greek Revival manner. Again, such attention to detail in a small house is rare, even today.

When I re-found the Woods House in 1958, it was in poor but not serious condition. I started the rehabilitation with the help of many friends; it was to be used for weekend retreats, since it offered a good change climatically from San Francisco. We began by applying paint. The roofs as well as the side walls were painted white to reflect the hot summer sun and also to give a kind of wedding-cake look; but, more important, white emphasized the form of the basic house.

The interior needed more than white paint. The front rooms were covered in a dismal flowered paper and the basic walls were too rough to paper over. So we tore off the newish paper and stretched mattress ticking over the walls, using a very narrow, subtle stripe. The edges were covered with tiny battens ($\frac{1}{2}''$ × $\frac{3}{4}''$) painted to match the darker color of the stripe (see picture). Thus, the look of the old house was preserved. Then the living room was simply painted a gold yellow to accent the door and window detail, and floors were covered with rush squares.

The old design of the Woods House also provided basic comfort. The box form is about fourteen feet high, leaving ten-feet-six-inch ceilings and a very sizable attic space. The high ceilings, attic and covered porch combined to make this house fifteen to twenty degrees cooler inside than out. On a hot summer day, if windows were left open on the north side, a cool breeze kept the house comfortable all day without an air conditioner!

This was to be used as a weekend house, and since my friends and I are not interested in living in the past, the furnishings mixed old and new. My primary profession is the creative design of new buildings; to live in the past is not appropriate in any way. Enjoying a fine old house for its basic beauty is perfectly rational if we do not slavishly try to re-create a past era to live in.

Many fine houses are to be found in the Gold Country, but none that I have seen express quite so well the remarkable relationship between basic forms of a structure for living—a house, plus added detailed refinements and considerations for comfort—even to its site on top of a knoll to provide views and cooling breezes. The Woods House is outstanding among houses of the period anywhere in this country. To repeat, I have, in fact, never seen a more interesting small house in America, be it in the North, East or the Old South.

The Woods House in Mokelumne Hill is east of the old Hotel Leger at 8014 Prospect Street, a very narrow street possibly best approached from the south end of town. As you will see on the map, Mokelumne Hill is just off the regular Route 49, though of course it was once on 49 and has only recently been bypassed to accommodate higher speeds.

You will find other houses in Mokelumne Hill worth seeing, too.

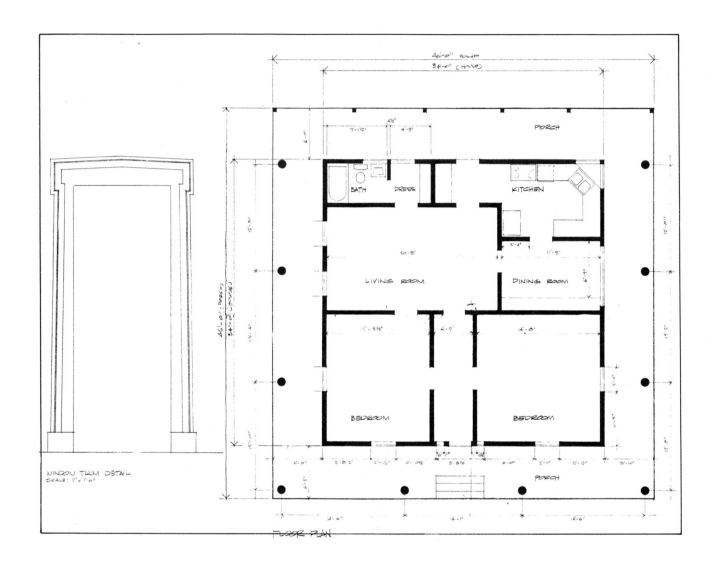

WINDOW TRIM DETAIL
SCALE: 1" = 1'-0"

FLOOR PLAN

Here, also, note the drawings and plan. Though not as detailed as with the Cady House, it does give an idea of the size. The house area was only 34 × 34 feet, the whole area, with porch, was 46 × 46 feet; so the living area was 1,156 sq. ft. compared to 1,600 sq. ft. in the Cady House.

SKETCH BY BETTY HAMILTON—1960

This photo was taken by the author in May 1939. At that time the house had shutters on the front door as well as on the windows. Paint had nearly washed off and the condition was run-down.

MORLEY BAER

The restored house painted all white, including the roof, to reflect the sun. The finial is a modern touch in gold leaf, added to cap the pyramid form.

PETER
MILLER
ARCHITECTURE
and DESIGN
BOOKS
1909 First
Avenue at Stewart
Seattle, WA. 98101

623-5563

see of Gold	15	00
TAX		98
TOTAL	15	98

/2/

PHOTO, CAMPBELL 1939

MORLEY BAER

Another 1939 picture, no column bases and clean detail.

Same look 20 years later. Columns apparently rotted out and bases were added. Observe the lack of finish under roof. Part of the charm of this house is the combination of roughness and refinement.

PHOTO CAMPBELL 1939

MORLEY BAER

Photo taken in 1939. Note: columns not truly vertical; old shutter on front door; no trim on stair.

Observe that the same columns are still out of line in 1959—and doubtless they still are in the 1980s.

SKETCH BY AUTHOR DONE IN 1939 FROM
MEMORY (WINDOWS AND COLUMNS NOT ACCURATE.)

A closer look showing the Victorian icicle detail
at the roof and the arch that connects the
battens. Notice the scale of the battens. These
are over planks two inches thick by six
inches wide. The Doric columns and caps
here are more purely Greek Revival than the
post and tops at the Cady House in Sonora.
Notice also the baseboard that gives a defined
finish to the cube form as it meets the floor.
A band like this is seldom seen in a small
wooden house. Also note that the porch edge
and steps are not as detailed as the rest of
the house.

Simple study of shutter column and lamp.

MORLEY BAER

MORLEY BAER

Detail of the ogee arches as a refined
finish for the battens, plus icicles
on every other batten.

Front door—fresh, crisp, inviting,
but old. Two lamps added.

Front door interior—original
paper in tatters, but left as evidence
of the way the house was built
(rough wood, stretched cheesecloth
and paper). Shows inside venting
window.

The living room adapted to
weekend use is a mix of old and
new, keeping the fine trim and
using plain-colored walls to accent
it. The chairs are 1850 desk
chairs, but the rest is new.

Enfilade—a French architectural term for seeing room after room through an opening; showing here the repeat of the classic door trim. The hallway wallpaper is the original.

MORLEY BAER

The bedroom with its elegant French doors. This house had no
windows, only doors.

This is the Schrag House as restored in the 70s. All of its original style is intact and it serves as well today as it did in the last century. The house was built in the 1860s by Kaufman Hexter as a gift to his son and his new bride. Here the three-sided porch occurs again. In 1909 it was sold furnished for $750.00— doubtless a proper price in that day.

These photos are from the Irma schrag Collection. She and a sister, Ruth, were raised in this house and moved to San Francisco upon their maturation. The horseman is Henry Schrag, their father. Other relatives are posed by the gate.

PHOTO IRMA SCHRAG

The Schrag house as restored in the 1970s is barely
changed from its original look. Here again is
Greek Revival trim around the windows.

This series of photos (taken in 1939 by the author) is not included for its photographic quality, but because newer ones are not available. The house is now vine-covered and does not reveal the architectural detail.

Grace Tallon House. This classic house at 115 Broadway St. is one of the most handsome in the Gold Country. It is basically the same as the Woods House in Mokelumne Hill—a cube, or box, structure with a pyramid roof and three-sided porch—but the detail is different. Tall, thin double columns and simpler detail at the eaves are the main differences. It has the same tall elegant French doors and shutters that work. In 1939 (when these photos were taken) I talked to the residents, who said the house had to be adapted from caprentry books brought from New England at the time. Here again, the simple carpenters' details are regrouped into a house fitting the Mother Lode climate.

PHOTO, CAMPBELL 1939

PHOTO, CAMPBELL 1939

PHOTO, CAMPBELL 1939

This snapshot gives a close-up of
the refined detail, the fine proportion,
and the simple material, all wood.

115 Broadway (In 1936 it was
36 Broadway.) A view of the entry.

PHOTO, CAMPBELL 1939

PHOTO, CAMPBELL 1939

The rear of the house, while not so elegant as the front, still has a turned spindle railing and a porch for protection from the sun. The more elegant double columns have turned into single posts.

Here is a third version of the same theme with the combination of pyramid roof and the cube forms and protective porch. However, the purity of the pyramid is topped with a rail, chimney and dormer. The roof is tin made to look like tile. The proportions of the house are not as elegant. The walls are stucco made to look like stone. It is (or was) a pleasant old house but it is not the classic that the Woods House or 115 Broadway is. This house was photographed in 1939 and I cannot locate it. It may be there, it may not, but I feel compelled to include it because of its interesting relationship to the Woods House and 115 Broadway in this same area.

The Armistead Brown House, 225 Church Street, Jackson. Built
in 1859. This fine old house is now a museum and is a good
example of its period with its double (or coupled) columns. Side-
lighted front door and symmetrical façade certainly symbols of
social stability. The two cedar trees in front were planted 116 years
ago. It was owned by the Brown family until 1949.

SUTTER CREEK

Sutter Creek is one of the least changed towns on Route 49 and the houses we show here are all on the main street. There are several excellent examples of the early period and most appear to fit the 1860s building types. They are consistent and well related to each other, all reflect the early design that is more Gold Rush than Victorian. The Main Street vista resembles the 1860s and 70s more than any other gold town, since most have been modernized with attendant loss of originality. Some balconies have been added here and there in recent years, but they are in the spirit of the original townscape.

A small house, built in 1858 by
John Keyes, is now an inn.
The Greek Revival front has, in this
case an added bay window.

A small house of pleasant
proportions with all the typical
Gold-Country earmarks:
three-sided porch, coupled columns
and small clapboard siding.

Sutter Creek, one of a row of houses on Main Street that expresses the classic Gold-Country style. This whole street is a rare example of many houses of consistent character in one place.

Yet another in the pattern. All are related, but each differs from the others in size of plan. Unity and variety are the result.

COLOMA
PLACERVILLE

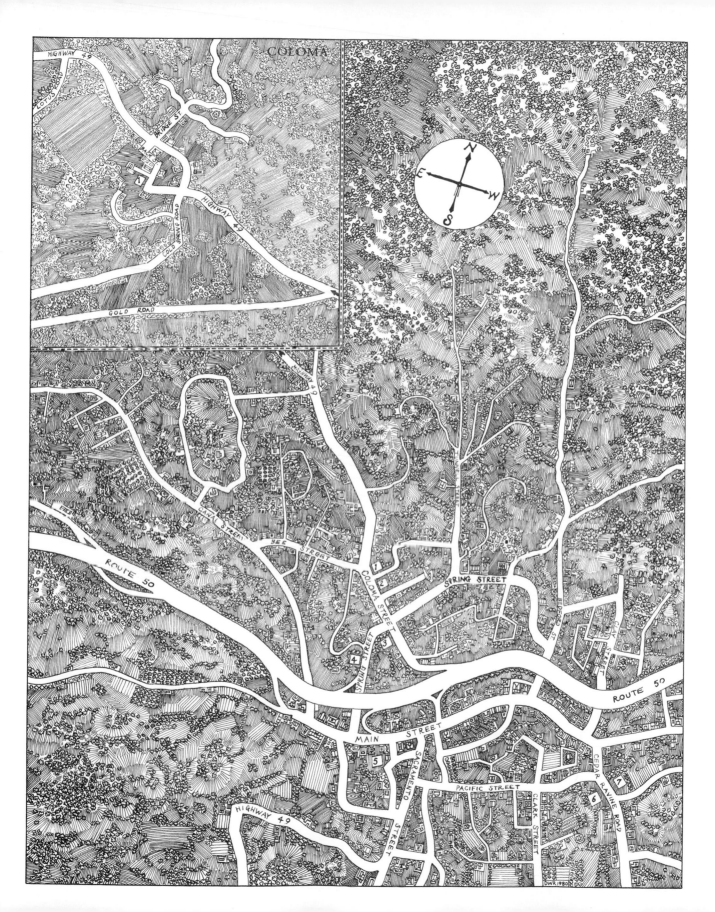

The Combellack House, Cedar Ravine. A vigorous
Victorian, replete with a tower, fanciful detail
and the large scale of the period. It surely expresses the
vitality of a way of life that was vigorous affluent
and house proud.

Combellack House tower.

Some detail from the Combellack

Here we add some stained glass.

The barn was done in by a heavy snow. The Gold Country varies from 1,500 ft. elevation to about 3,500 ft. so that the snow loads vary north to south. For instance, it snows in Nevada City several times a season, almost always lightly; however only five miles away it can be very heavy.

Many of the buildings in the 1850 to 1900 period didn't make it to the 20th Century except as ruins or sawdust. We see here the process—first the roof goes, then the walls collapse, unprotected from the ravages of sun and storms; however, they make beautiful ruins if they're stone.

❻

Blair House. 3062 Cedar Ravine. Built in 1863. Across the street from the Combellack House is Blair House. This house is quite similar to the Coleman House in Grass Valley, though not as complex or as large. The entry hall features original 111-year-old Chinese Dado wallpaper. Huge ballroom, 15′ × 27′, later used by the Judge as a law library. Beautiful dining room with ornate chandelier. Downstairs bath features antique tin bathtub. The grounds have a parkline setting with numerous fruit trees, and lush shrubs that are up to 100 years old. Peaceful Hang-town Creek flows beneath the dining room and outside deck. Built in 1963 by Mr. and Mrs. John Blair, and was occupied by them until 1982, at which time it was rented by the Anderson family, until Judge Thompson married their daughter Gertrude and then purchased the home in 1905.

Chichester House, a Victorian house—all
three porches appear to be of later date. The
material and the angles of the porches,
and the spacing of supports, does not seem
consistent with the period.

A small Victorian house interesting for the combination of forms—
the finial on the tower and the corner brackets by the bay window.

⑤

Fausel House in Placerville. One of the few brick houses, interesting because the usable outdoor space (the balcony) is on the second floor. This is one of the most attractive houses in the area.

❶

COLOMA

A small house in Coloma. (Near the site of the discovery of gold.)
The bargeboard is a nice contrast to the otherwise simple structure.
The shutter work and Greek Revival trim are seen on the front
porch only. The railing does not look like it is original to the house.
The narrow lap siding is another element typical of the earlier
Gold Rush houses.

PLACERVILLE

Jaeger House. Much simpler than
most; it would look contemporary
with shingles and detail removed.

AUBURN

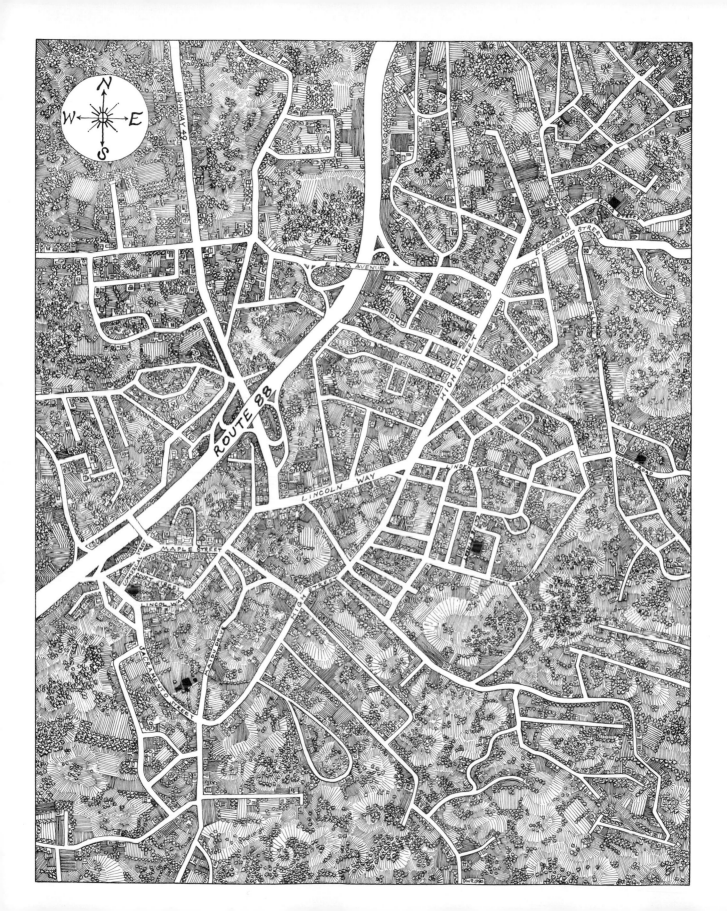

Bernhard House. Here is a remarkable complex of buildings consisting of: a fine house, a stone warehouse in front and a brick outbuilding to the rear. The house is in the early Gold Rush tradition. Much like buildings in New England with narrow clapboard siding, but the porch is a California addition. Simple eave and facia detail and small windows evenly spaced in the walls. During its restoration one could see the once typical structure—narrow exterior siding, rough interior boards of slab dimensions over studs, then on top of that cheesecloth stretched and papered.

The Bernhard House is one of the finest buildings in the Gold Country and of special interest because of the relationship of the house was built in 1851 as a travelers rest and served as a hotel until Mr. and Mrs. Bernhard bought it to use as a house in 1868. The surrounding lands were vineyards and a mulberry grove that fed a silk industry.

The house is unusual in the location of the handsome porch, which was probably originally used to accommodate arrivals and departures when it served as a hotel. It is now being restored by the Placer County Historic Museum Park, and the work is being done by Architects Jon and George Lardner. A most commendable effort by all parties.

The passageway between the house and the stone warehouse reveals
the golden dome of the county seat, and conversely beneath
the ground here is a tunnel passage between house and warehouse.

The north side showing the brick
outbuilding which was a blacksmith
shop.

BRIEF HISTORY OF PROJECT SITE OF THE BERNHARD HOUSE

The Old Auburn Historic District-Travelers Rest has been designated as a site on the National Register of Historic Places and is listed on the Inventory of Historic Features of the California History Plan. The site is being restored and developed as the Placer County Historical Museum Park.

Historically the Travelers Rest site is significant for several reasons. The Travelers Rest, built in 1851, is Auburn's only surviving hotel of the early Gold Rush. The land adjoining, west of the site originally known as Rich Flat, was rich in gold and extensively worked by the early miners.

In 1868 Benjamin and Rosa Bernhard purchased the Travelers Rest and surrounding thirty acres and developed the property successfully as a vineyard, fruit ranch, winery and distillery. They also planted 1,000 mulberry trees and experimented in silk production. The "well-directed industry" of these German immigrants brought forth the agricultural "wealth of the foothill land" on this heretofore mining site.

The Bernhards occupied the Travelers Rest as their family home and constructed a winery and blacksmith shop. These buildings remain, in various states of deterioration. Other buildings which they built, including a stable and a distillery, have been destroyed since their deaths in 1902. A biographical sketch of the Bernhards is included in Thompson and West's 1882, *History of Placer County*.

Most of the original thirty acres owned by the Bernhards became part of the Twentieth District Agricultural Fairgrounds in 1957. In 1973, two acres of the site including the Travelers Rest Residence, Winery and Blacksmith Shop was deeded to Placer County for the purpose of restoring and developing this site as the Placer County Historical Museum Park.

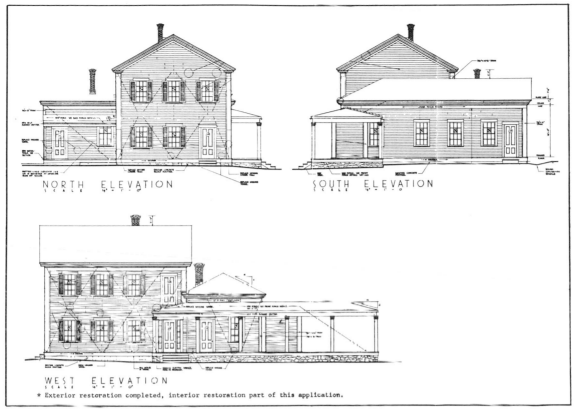

NORTH ELEVATION
SCALE ¼" = 1'-0"

SOUTH ELEVATION
SCALE ¼" = 1'-0"

WEST ELEVATION
SCALE ¼" = 1'-0"

* Exterior restoration completed, interior restoration part of this application.

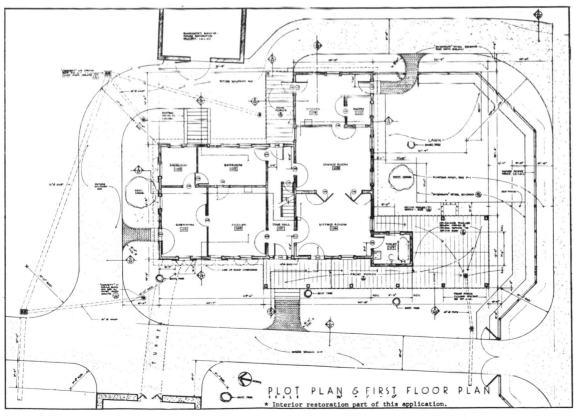

PLOT PLAN & FIRST FLOOR PLAN
SCALE ¼" = 1'-0"

* Interior restoration part of this application.

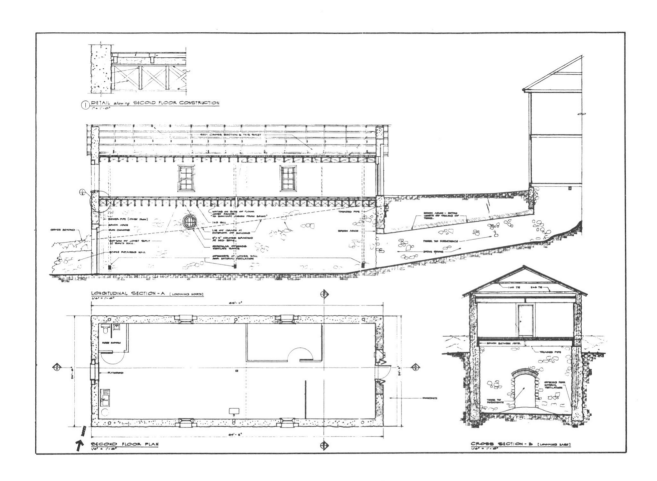

1 DETAIL showing SECOND FLOOR CONSTRUCTION

LONGITUDINAL SECTION - A [LOOKING NORTH]

SECOND FLOOR PLAN

CROSS SECTION - B [LOOKING EAST]

Bayley House, built in 1862, is one of the few
houses we see that can be called a mansion
for sheer size as well as elegance. It is comparable
to some Southern Mansions, though not as
large. Unfortunately it is now in a sad state of
disrepair and desperately needs restoring.

An unusual house not typical of any of the others, but related to all
of them—that is to say the form is more Victorian than the
earliest house, but it is much simpler than the usual Victorians. The
most interesting detail of this house is the Gothic windows.—
Owned now by Jon Lardner of the team of architects restoring
the Bernhard house, located at 235 Olive Street.

The major gable with varied-shingle pattern, some Gothic window detail and a small detail on the gable facia board.

The small dormer that is not really a dormer, but here accents the windows below. We can see the restrained detail over the Gothic arches.

225 Aeolia Street. Another large Victorian, consistent in its large scale.

More Victorian detail—never-ending variations on a theme—
ornate, consistent, but not repetitive.

A Gothic Revival house in wood with
three-sided porch; bargeboard is interesting.

The Butterworth House, just above Old Town, a handsomely
simple building with shutters added, however, they will not close
over the windows. (Better they be left off if they do not serve a
constructive purpose). The iron railing on the steps is not original
in feeling either, but the overall proportion and the porch detail
make a distinctive house. This house is now a restaurant.

A snapshot of a group of miner's shacks in a row. They were possibly part of a small settlement along a stream where there was gold.

A house in the earliest times of the Gold Rush. Steep roof to shed snow—rather pleasant proportions, but totally unrefined as in later houses in the Gold Country.

192 Lubeck Road. A fine house, again with shutters added for looks and not function, and an iron rail that doesn't help either. Still, it is a well proportioned structure in a fine setting, and the overall effect is handsome.

GRASS VALLEY

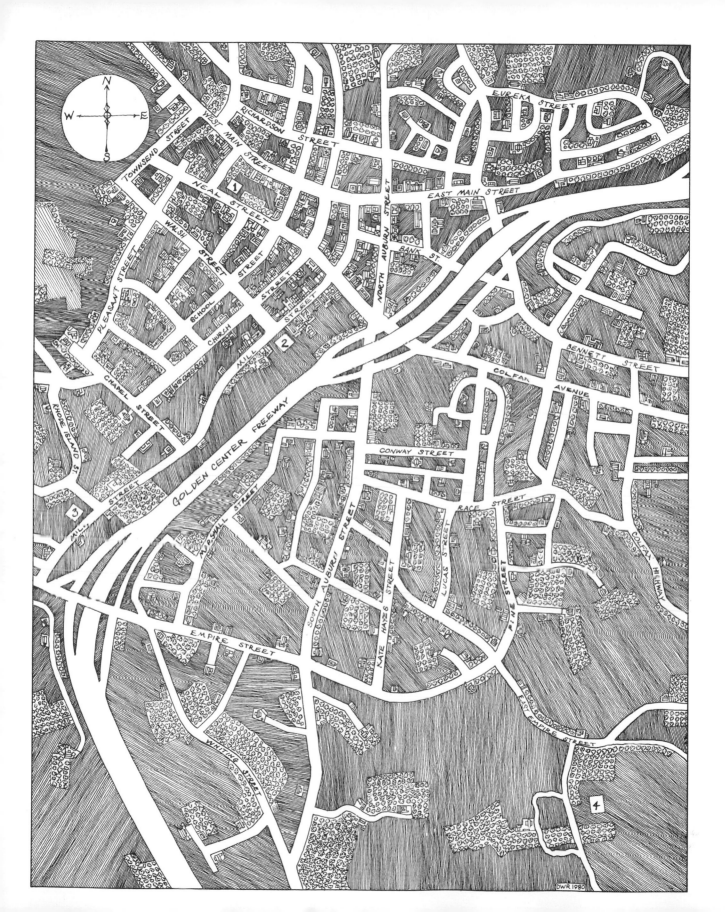

Coleman House

Grass Valley,
111 Neal Street
Here is one of the most
handsome houses in
the Gold Country. A
classic example of sym-
metry, bold forms,
refined detail, elegant
proportions and
remarkable simplicity.
A major aspect of this
house is its
maintenance. It is
always in top
condition—fresh, crisp
and white and the

carefully trained ivy is
also an unusual visual
part of the house.
Topiary is seldom seen
in use this way—to
enhance a building
directly. We more often
see topiary used to
imitate birds, animals
or abstract forms in a
garden. You will see,
by comparing the old
print with the new
photo, that the house
has been maintained
throughout the years.

The curve of the
segmented arch on the
upper bay window is
repeated by the curved
supports on the porch.
This house, as do
others, includes the
three basic design
elements—curves, as
just mentioned; straight
lines in the basic
structure; and angles
in the diamond-
patterned lattice below
the porch.

From the same angle on the old print.

Detail of the bay combining angles, curves and straight lines.

Stair and rail detail

Side view of Coleman House

A detail of the porch reemphasizes
the pleasant proportions and
contrast of white paint and green ivy.

GRASS VALLEY

A small cottage, simple to be sure, but built of
beautiful stone.

3

GRASS VALLEY

A large house for its time—interesting
symmetrical window placement.

4

A stone-and-brick mansion on the Empire Mine grounds designed by Willis Polk in 1898. This house is an exception to all the others, but since it was produced by gold, it is part of the House of Gold idea. It is totally unlike any other of the houses of the period, giving the effect of a European lodge rather than an American house. However it is well worth seeing. The combination of rough stone and the more refined brick is unusual. The area is a state park open to the public.

An entrance detail showing the careful and skillfully designed brick-and-stone combination.

NEVADA CITY

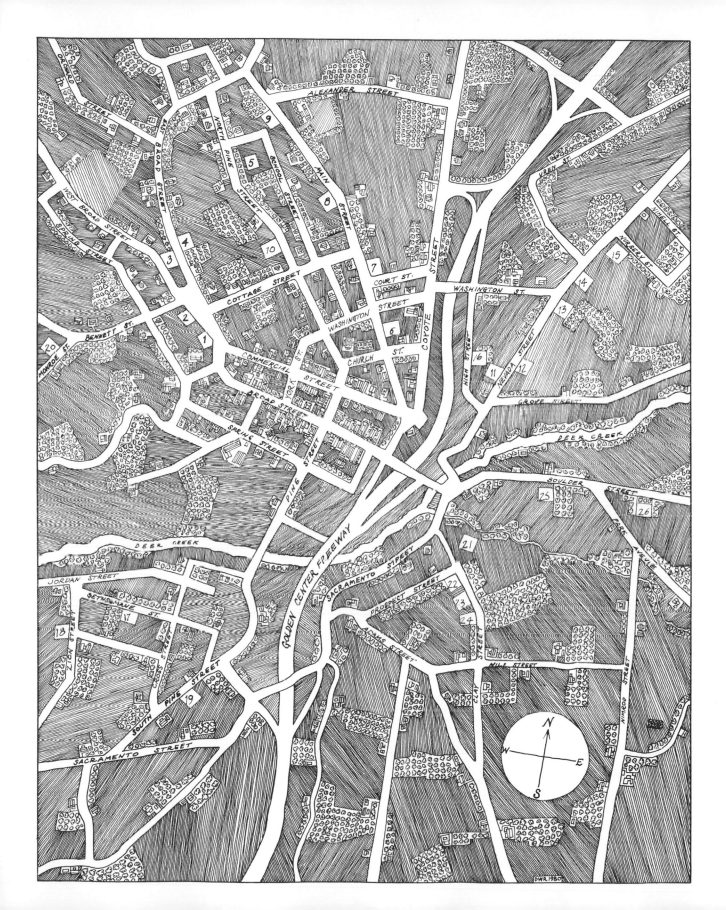

An overview of the town showing the forest terrain and the changes in architecture on the main street—everything from the 1860s theatre (recently retrieved from a modern stucco front) to an Art Deco city hall, to typical gable-roof small shops.

Bourbon Lodge at 236 Nevada Street, owned today by Freeman and Marling, original builder unknown. Reputed to be oldest frame in Nevada City. Built in 1852–53.

I believe this to be one of the most handsome houses in the whole Gold Country – truly simple Greek Revival detail and form, and eminently suited to the climate and terrain. Pass Christian and Biloxi on the Gulf Coast of Alabama have houses like this that look out to the beaches and gulf. It is interesting to note that while the columns are evenly spaced and symmetrical, the front door is off-center.

History says this was originally built as a club for the more elegant gents to avoid the cruder aspects of the early Gold Rush days . . . and it is on Aristocracy Hill! It, nonetheless, has been a gracious house for generations.

Detail of the porch, illustrating a
sense of leisure and refinement.

17

The Katherine Cello Gibbons House, 315 Gethsemane. Another of the simple classics. The symmetrical front is interestingly set "off" by a widened front panel door. The wood-quoined corners (as in the Marsh and Bartlett Houses) are in imitation of stone. The tall, elegant proportions distinguish this house from the usual box. True here, and in most of these houses, the ample lawns and foliage make them all the more appealing. Built in 1885 by Robert Forman, a carriage builder from New York.

The Gibbons iron garden fence—a fine piece of end of the century decoration.

449 Broad Street. Built in 1856 for Senator A. A. Sargent. Another very good example of the mixing and blending of two ideas or styles. A simple rectangular box for living with a restrained amount of Victorian detail (often called Gingerbread). Here the long horizontal emphasis of the porch gives this house a very special character. Where the American Gothic several doors down expresses the vertical direction, this house has the horizontal emphasis —even the window divisions are in horizontal lines. Again, fence and landscaping add to its overall consistent character.

Note front door detail: columns and
elaborate caps.

Detail of the upper bay. Note the
Gothic arch used here in the railing.

447 Broad Street. A real piece of "American Gothic," as Grant Wood might have called this simple style of house. It is, in fact, another example of Victorian proportion and Greek Revival simplicity, blended to its own style in California foothills. The doorway and the mid-story tall French doors give elegance to this small house.

Next door to our American Gothic, not as elegant in proportion, but interesting in detail. Observe the tiny edging on the gable board.

This early house is often referred to as Italianate—probably because
of the split columns with arched tops. It has all of the classic
elements of its time—the tall French doors, the three-sided porch,
narrow clapboard siding—but it has a tower that is not
typical. Some say this was added after the main house was built.

The Red Castle seen among the tall green cedars and pines. It is a house similar to the Ben Thorne House in San Andreas. Three-story brick with detail at the gable ends and the porch on three sides, again, for shade from the summer heat. This house is now a hotel furnished with antiques that suit the house. Prospect and Clay.

The William Morris Stewart House, home of a senator, built in 1855. The south wing was added in 1898. This is doubtless one of the finest examples of Greek Revival in the Gold Country. A two-story house, with an unrailed balcony that is apparently not meant to be used. The two-tiered columns are the only ones we know of that are constructed in this manner. Zion Street.

⓬

216 Nevada Street. Naffziger House, built by Charles Kent in 1859.
Almost neighbor to the valentined house is this simple house.
Note the pure arched window with usable shutters, a handsome
doorway, a curved railing and roof leads us to a wing where the
house becomes two stories. Note again the narrow clapboard
as in the Cady House.

309 Park Avenue—a Victorian with rich detail and with the typical asymmetrical façade; a nice iron fence rail and a large stone wall below (built approximately 1890 by Dr. Shaw).

A close-up of some of the playful detail. Note particularly the patterned cut board under the window—it is unlike any I have seen anywhere; and the trim by the glass door repeats in variation the post detail

The fancy gable, complete with sunburst, expresses the exuberance of much of Victorian, as opposed to the more sedate and restrained qualities of the earlier houses. The owners could afford more, so they just added it on to their houses.

More of the same.

224 High Street. Bennett House.
One of the larger houses in Nevada City and again really interesting for its fusion of styles. The bay window is Victorian; the tall window and the second floor resemble the earlier styles. Also the two-story columns are used here in a way I have not seen anywhere else in Gold Country. They seem more like devices for formality and elegance, because they do not support any functional porch for example. A truly handsome house.

509 N. Pine.
Another example of the pleasant
combination of 1850s and 1880s.

Porch detail showing interesting
columns.

14

Haley House, 304 Nevada Street. Yet another
combination of a simple form, much
enriched with textures and patterns. The upper
part has always reminded me of a charming
valentine.

Here we can study the details and
note the interesting Gothic arch of
the window and its usable matching
shutters.

23

212 Clay. Built by Williamson about 1895. Another Victorian, replete with lots of texture, fanciful posts and railings, large-scale forms and asymmetry. This still has its original hitching post for horses.

A close-up of the details.

15

NEVADA CITY

The Rector House, owned by generations of the Rector family. This house is a real classic of the Victorian tradition in that it had a garden as splendid as the house. In the spring and summer it is a study in green and white with rolling lawn and tall old trees of various kinds. Built by Dr. R. M. Hunt in 1885. 316 Nevada.

24

Bartlett House, 218 Clay Street, Nevada City. Built in the late 1870s by M. L. Marsh. This house is very much like the Marsh House. A large cube form embellished with simple detail. One could say Victorian, but it's a far cry from the Rector House or the F. W. Street House. It has the quoined corners and a belvedere of arched windows and eave brackets like the Marsh House. Here it should be noted that the porch was redone like in the 1970s. It may have had a full porch like the Marsh House, but that was replaced with a clipped-eave narrow porch. Then this was redesigned and reroofed to be more in keeping with the rest of the old houses. It has two magnificent magnolia trees flanking the entry.

A handsome house at 308 Broad Street. A flat front broken with three bays of different size. The use of the pediment again, and again different from others. This house was once the home of the Mein family, now prominent San Franciscans.

A fine simple
Victorian that needs a
little restoration.
You will notice in the
old print that
there was a handsome
porch on the side.
This apparently dete-
riorated, was torn
off and replaced with
a small shed
roof. Functional to be
sure, but it is not
appropriate to
the dignity of the old
house. Main and
Church Street.

NEVADA CITY

Mulloy House, East & West Broad Street. Looking up Broad Street where it divides, we see another enriched box or cube. But here a fanciful tower is placed over the door, second-floor bay, and on top of the roof. The effect is strongly interesting, because it some-how does not seem very residential. Built about 1870.

Close-up of the tower with its turned wood finial; a cone resting on four triangles that are supported by a cube. Three basic forms, but not as purely executed as in the Wood House.

The cone form again, but note that the finial is different.

Close-ups of gable details, Victorian variety seems infinite. . .

A gable detail with the usual playfulness—three kids of shingle cuts: round, angle and straight (three basic design elements) are combined in a really small area.

NEVADA CITY

414 Main Street. An example of Victorian that is particularly simple. No gingerbread, and the two-story bay dominates the house. The segmented arched windows are unornamented. The boxed-in part of the porch on the right was added in recent years.

Small house on Boulder Street, with the now typical small clapboard sides, porch and functional shutters.

9

A cottage in size, but the porch and shutters
give it a distinction; the hedge of green texture
completes the picture. 561 Main Street.

Another Victorian—blend of early simplicity,
later complexity.

A large scale Victorian, with complex details.

⑲

A small house but with the coupled columns,
tall windows and porch on the side. It fits the
prototype developed out of the time and the
climate. Also pre-Victorian. 421 S. Pine Street.

211 Nevada Street. An unusually small Victorian with less
detail than most, but still an inviting house. It is doubtful that the
large lower front window is original, since windows of that
size and proportion were not typical of the period. No date available.

5

Another early classic —the ever-present three-sided porch. By now
we see it as a typical architectural device to solve a problem.
The large bay was added in the 1970s. Pine and School Street.

The Marsh-Christie House*

254 Boulder Street
Nevada City

Martin Luther Marsh, born in Middletown, Ohio, in 1831, came to California in 1850. He spent time in Sacramento, Nevada City and Iowa Hill before settling permanently in Nevada City in 1859. His business enterprises did so well that in 1862 he traveled to the East, returning late the same year by way of the Isthmus of Panama on the clipper ship *Orizaba*.

On the same ship, Emma Ann Ward was traveling from Wisconsin with her mother and sister to join her father in Santa Cruz. After a two-year courtship, Emma Ann married Martin Luther and came to Nevada City in 1864 to a new home on Park Avenue.

By the 1860s, Nevada City was still a young but important town in the Northern Mines. In 1867, Marsh purchased the lot for a new house from Charles Young; six years later, in the spring of 1873, construction began. The design of the house was taken from Sloan's *The Model Architect,* a Victorian pattern book published in 1852.

The house Marsh built for his wife is a formal rendition of the Victorian-Italianate style, translated by local builders into a unique, well-detailed Gold Country villa. Design details of the exterior are typically Classic in style; they are nominally "Italianate" because their origins are in renditions of Classic buildings in Renaissance Italy. Such details were used on buildings in Europe and America from the 16th through the 19th centuries.

The house itself is a formal symmetrical building surmounted by a hip-roofed cupola with arched windows reminiscent of Roman arcaded arches. The individual elements consist of a heavy cornice with

*Information about the Marsh-Christie House is taken from the brochure of The American Victorian Museum, Nevada City.

strongly modeled brackets; heavily sculptured wood pediments over the windows, a vestige of the pediment on a Classic Greek Temple; imitation beveled stone quoins at the corners of the building; pine siding on the front, scored to simulate stone. The plan of the house consists of a formal arrangement of central hall, central stairway, four principal rooms on each floor and a kitchen at the rear—a typical plan of Colonial and Federal houses.

Martin Luther Marsh, a carpenter before coming to California, was a lumberman; his lumberyard was across Boulder Street from "The Big House." The interior sugar-pine woodwork in the house is a tribute to his taste and to the skill and judgment of the builders. The materials used in construction are all native: foundations of quarried rock held in a lime-and-sand mortar; inner foundation walls of local brick; cedar and red fir beams, some as long as 32 feet.

Four generations of the Marsh family lived in the house. Although formal in concept, it reflects all of the varied tastes and lives of those who lived there. It was never static—not a Victorian house crystallized in a single date or moment—but was lived in by real people. So the chandelier in the library would have been a hundred-year-old antique hung by the Marshes in the new room, and the curtains would have been modern replacements for worn Victorian ones.

In 1954, Lucille Marsh Christie, a granddaughter of M. L. Marsh, returned to Nevada City. With her husband, James, she restored and rebuilt the home as it now stands. A woman of great style and good taste, she gathered as many authentic artifacts and furnishings as possible for the restoration, creating a fine document of the past. It is one of the most impressive reminders of residential design and construction in the Northern Mines, and with careful attention to interior furnishings, recaptures for the visitor the atmosphere of that earlier period. Mrs. Christie deserves to be honored for this restoration and also for her dedicated help in other preservation efforts in Nevada City, notably the theatre.

I am happy to say that I attended the 100th birthday of the Marsh-Christie House in October 1973, when Mrs. Christie hosted a sit-down dinner in the rear garden for one hundred seventy-five guests—a gala event for a truly rare occasion. So few of us can celebrate the 100th birthday of the house we live in that we have cause to cherish those old houses still remaining.

A year after Lucille Christie's death, the house was acquired by The American Victorian Museum for use as a living Nineteenth Century Exhibit House. Thus it remains a living tribute to Mrs. Christie and her devotion to preserving historic buildings in a sensitive, tasteful manner.

Interior details of the Marsh-Christie House are worthy of note:

The Music Room. Nineteenth Century square grand piano; Victorian reed organ originally from Nevada City (loaned by Karen and Mel Locher of Auburn).

The Study. Rare book collection from the 19th Century Research Library of The American Victorian Museum; Marsh Family memorabilia.

Dining Room. Collection of paintings and prints from the 19th Century, principally given by Dr. Joseph A. Baird, Jr.

Front Bedroom. The Eastlake Suite loaned by the Searls Family from the historic Niles Searls House, Nevada City.

East Bedroom. Original sleigh bed and Victorian furniture.

West Bedroom. The historic master-bedroom suite from bonanza king James L. Flood's Linden Towers in San Mateo.

Playroom. Games, puzzles, toys and paintings from The American Victorian Museum collection.

Bathroom. Original porcelain water closet from Legg & Shaw, Nevada City; original tin bathtub.

Trunk Room. Nineteenth Century quilts and fabrics, including a rare Jacquard loom coverlet and a knitted spread in shell or fan pattern from Virginia, c. 1840.

The Marsh-Christie House is open to the public by appointment only, so be sure to check with The American Victorian Museum.

A handsome, strong and symmetrical façade described in the notes; but be sure to compare this actual wooden house with the historic plate from Sloan's *Model Architect* published in 1852. You can see the difference in proportion and material (the Sloan House in stone, the March House in wood). Do read the description from the old plate.

Two façades of the Sloan—the Model Architect description of this design.

The Marsh House was adapted from these two houses—made to relate to the Sierra Foothills and available material—wood.

A PLAIN VILLA.

THE SAME ORNAMENTED.

case the work be at a distance or so extensive as to require constant attendance, that the owner need make the transfer. If there are any reservations made by either party, they should be endorsed upon the articles of agreement. The security of the party of the first part is in the same form as that given, the names of the parties being reversed. When the work is complete, it is essential that the owner receive a release "of all claims, liens, or charges whatsoever," signed by each and every person who either may have furnished material for the building, or who may have done any labor in its erection; otherwise, after the business between himself and the contractor be finally closed, he may be compelled to liquidate claims which the other has failed to discharge.

The business of entering into and fulfilling such a contract is by no means easy, and inexcusable carelessness in this is the cause of innumerable lawsuits. By using the above form, and exercising judgment and care in its adaptation, no difficulty need be apprehended.

A PLAIN AND ORNAMENTED VILLA.
DESIGN ELEVENTH.

Two front elevations of this design are presented on plates XLVIII. and XLIX. They are spoken of as the same design, because their breadth, depth, and general features are similar, and the same floor plans are used for both. The first of these elevations is quite plain, being almost destitute of ornament, but at the same time so finished as to avoid a barren appearance. The second on the other hand is highly ornamented, and a half story higher than the first, thus giving a commodious garret, the circular windows of which may be seen over those of the second story. The observatory of this elevation is covered, and might be arranged without a floor, so as to give additional light and ventilation to the garret rooms. The garret or loft is approached in each by a flight of stairs, over those leading to the second story. The cellar door is beneath the main stairway, and the windows are on the sides of the building. The elevations are drawn in a scale of ten feet to the inch. The design is best adapted to a village or suburban dwelling. We have presented the extremes of plainness and decoration, so that any desirable medium may be attained.

On plate L. are the floor plans of the design. The house is intended to be warmed either by stoves or by a furnace beneath the hall. The flues for heated air are in the cross partitions, and the gas flues are at the sides of the building, giving a sufficient breadth of projection for mantles. The recess in the dining room, next the vestibule, is a convenient situation for a sideboard. The parlor and library are separated by sliding doors. It would be as well, perhaps, to reverse the steps and have them begin against the rear wall, thus presenting a better appearance from the hall. A convenient back porch might be placed in the rear or at the side of the kitchen, which might be built two stories high, and thus give an additional chamber. The two windows of the first and second story, in the rear of the stairway, serve to admit more light to the passage below and the hall above, but might be dispensed with.

The east side of the Marsh House shows a strong symmetrical elevation. The height of house is more evident here and indicates the height of the ceilings inside.

A view from the rear, including an adjacent outbuilding.

A view of the mahogany stair.

A collection of toys belonging to the American Victorian
Museum. Note the childrens' chairs and also the simple trim around
the windows.

A real gem, 1873 and still working, wooden seat and all. It is rare that we see such sculptural finery on such a humble, everyday piece of functional household equipment.

The old tin tub set in a paneled box and the corner basin. Note also the wood tongue-and-groove walls.

Front bedroom, reportedly occupied by a benign ghost. (I recently experienced a visit from the ghost when I slept in this very bed!)

Dining room, and a look into the library. This all is original to the house or of the period except for the light fixture, which appears to be somewhat out of character. Note the glass over the door and how it extends the proportion of the picture molding.

Front and rear parlors. Note the simple brick and wood
mantelpiece. It is interesting because most in this period (1813)
were marble.

Round-up

To walk through a square in Boston and see the Old North Church and Paul Revere on his bronze horse arouses a sense of history that is vitalizing. Just as rewarding is a walk through the French Quarter of New Orleans, or a drive down Chestnut Street in Salem, or an attempt to unriddle the reasons behind a Victorian façade.

Now an equally inviting experience awaits you: adventuring into the foothills of California to see, feel and sense the Houses of Gold.

Knowing we have a past is reassuring; it reminds us that we are all part of the ongoing human parade. As we walk through an historic village we can feel a sense of security in our ties to the past.

But we are living now, today, and we cannot live in the past. So let us look at these Houses of Gold with pleasure and interest, realizing that with the materials available and within the limits of their money and skills, our forebears developed many fine houses suited to their time. Like them, many of us today build houses that fit the times and the budget. Some, in fact, continue to use an old house for living, though usually renovating it to accommodate present lifestyle. (An historic house decorated exactly as it was when new is apt to look more like a museum than a home.) Houses change with new needs and skills, but the purposes remain much the same . . . to provide attractive, secure shelters for personal living. Thus we can thoroughly admire and appreciate these fine old houses, but not feel a need to copy them.

The old houses you will see in the Gold Country have many attributes and uses as historic documents: some have been converted into inns or have become museums; others are still being used as houses, much as they were one hundred years ago.

This "Look Book" guide will open your eyes to much more than houses, however. You will also discover that Route 49 through the Gold Country is one of the most rewarding areas in California in its combination of historic sites and buildings with beautiful landscapes and geological variety—all of this colored by seasonal changes. Spring green at the foothill altitude is fresh and exciting. Summer is usually dry and hot. Autumn's bright display may not be as abundant as in New England, but will please the fall-color enthusiast. Winter brings light snows to most of the area once or twice a year. Since the average elevation is between 1,500 and 2,500 feet, snow is seldom heavy or lasting. Of course, only another hour or so away is the High Sierra with real snow and sports.

The book starts with Sonora and goes north, though you could obviously start at Nevada City and go south. To help you plan your trip, you will find the book divided into four areas, relating loosely to the highways leading into the Gold Country. Route 108 (120) leads to Sonora; next north is Route 88, going into Jackson; further north is Route 50 through Placerville; and the most northerly is Route 80 through Auburn. Both 80 and 50 lead to Tahoe; 88 and 108 also go into the High Sierra. These four roads indicate the variety of approaches to Route 49 and the main track of our adventure from Sonora to Nevada City (although Route 49 continues south to Mariposa and north to Downieville).

Incidentally, most towns along the route offer good places to stay and interesting things to see and do in addition to looking at architecture. At this time the town that seems to offer the greatest variety for the traveler is Nevada City. You will find three or four excellent restaurants; the Red Castle is an historic place to stay; and various drinking establishments provide entertainment as well. There are several museums, including The American Victorian Museum, one firehouse, an historic foundry, many very good antique shops, and even rivers nearby for fishing and swimming—all this at a cool altitude of 2,500 feet.

Nevada City is built on eight hills, named Prospect, Piety, Aristocracy, Bourbon, Boulder, Oregon, Nabob and Lost Hills—all of them covered with houses of varying ages. You can see more old houses of quality in Nevada City than in any of the other gold towns, some of them the best to be found in the Gold Country. Nevada City has spent more effort on preservation than most towns, while still keeping up with the times. Here the past and present mingle comfortably, except possibly for the ugly slash of totally unnecessary freeway that splits the town in half.

We cannot say we have recorded every good house in the Gold Country, nor do we have a history of each one. We have included most of the best and have given histories of some, but information is not available for every house you can see. Our data has come through "oral history"—technically undocumented evidence, but told to us by persons knowledgeable in each case.

The real purpose of this book is to help you discover, on your own, houses that you may find as fascinating as the ones we have covered, making it a trip of discovery for all. So even though every house you see may not have a recorded history, you will find significance in studying the relationship of one house to another and their relationship to the period when each was built.

Be aware that a particular house or building may be played up because it once housed a famous person or was the scene of an historical event; but it may also be uninteresting architecturally, possibly even ugly. On the other hand, a very beautiful old building standing nearby may not have the same glamorous history. One is not better than the other, or worse; they mean different things to different people. So enjoy what you see without worrying whether Kit Carson or Joaquin Murietta did or did not sleep in the house—or rob the place.

This whole area teems with "history." The aura of a fascinating period in the building of the West is what enriches this region—not just any one house but the total feeling of the aftermath of the Gold Rush era.

The book has been planned like a treasure hunt—with some clues, but not all the answers. There are no planned tours. Some addresses are obscure or even missing, but the pictures will confirm your findings, and best of all you may find some favorites of your own. Enjoy your trip, be it from your car or your armchair.

THE HOUSES SHOWN IN THIS BOOK
ARE PRIVATE HOMES. PLEASE DO NOT
INVADE THEIR PRIVACY. THANK YOU.